The Shape of Emptiness

The Shape of Emptiness

poems

Regina O'Melveny

Sheila-Na-Gig Editions
Volume 3

Copyright © 2019, Regina O'Melveny

Author photo: Bill O'Melveny
Cover art: *Passageway*, a watercolor by Regina O'Melveny

ISBN PRINT: 9781732940642
ISBN EBOOK: 9781732940659

Published by Sheila-Na-Gig Editions
www.sheilanagigblog.com

ALL RIGHTS RESERVED
Printed in the United States of America

for Bill, Adrienne, Kaela & Charlie

ACKNOWLEDGMENTS

I am grateful to the editors of the following periodicals and the anthology in which some of these poems first appeared:

College English: "Swarms"
Crab Orchard Review: "Caps of Pure Silk"
The Ear: "The Bright New Dress and the Book about Jungles"
Explorations: "Ossa"
Kestrel: "Buzz Saw and Mockingbird," "Stars Burned in the Sky above Him," "The Finishing Stitches"
Passages North: "The Last Thing You See"
The Pittsburgh Quarterly: "A String Tied to Each Wrist"
Poetry New Zealand: "Cara Mamina"
Rattapallax: "Brussels Sprouts in Limbo"
Salt Hill Journal: "Off the Richter Scale," "The Bombardier"
Sheila-Na-Gig online: "The Origins of Language"
Whiskey Island: "Black Helicopters," "Formic Acid," "Middle Age and the Rings of Uranus," "Orb-Weaver," "Referred Pain"
Wisconsin Review: "Dog"
The Word Thursdays Anthology: "Lunch Tray"

"Funnel Spider," "Swarms," and "The Best Time to Plant" first appeared in my prizewinning chapbook *other gods* published by Southword Editions, Munster Literature Centre, Cork, Ireland.

CONTENTS

I. The Shape of Emptiness

The Annals of Wind

wind that apocalypses sun
turns desert to cloud
reverses time
empties the ears of desire

wind that spins the heart in its chambers
drinks the moisture of dreams
desiccates fear
does not stir a hair
provokes the trees against gravity

wind that combs sadness from elderly scalps
frees prisoners
clamps the doors shut
copulates

wind that hums underwater
drives splinters into memory remembers
your grandmother's kisses gets lost in
the dark
curses the gods

wind that sings scythes
concludes the ashes
aches with providence
squawks at toll takers

wind that speaks through the mouths of dead children
murmurs under your tongue
goes home empty-handed
defeats bullets
dances the skeletons

wind

Night

I don't turn on the heat in the cold house.
Better to learn the season in my bones.

The chalk point of a star scratches
my course across slate heaven.

The window holds cedar branches against
the failed darkness of urban sky.

I can't see the desert that lies to the east, the
place where the moon leaves no doubt.

The poem, a bezoar stone, accretes in my gut,
hair, seeds, husks, old loves that won't dissolve.

Brassica raposa

Most nights now, I fall asleep gazing at plants painted by
an unknown hand in sixteenth-century Netherlands.

My sadness settles, a tiny black insect among
the rhizomes, leaves and flowers.

The watercolors gathered by Theodorus Clutius
once served *in winter in lieu of the garden.*

In the herbarium all seasons were one,
bud, flower, fruit on the selfsame plant.

Four centuries later the garden was lost during WW II,
until at last the pages surfaced in Poland.

The plant names in fine script, noted locale,
temperament and seasons in six distinct languages,

with English pleasantly absent,
a fine respite from supremacy.

I yearn for such a subtle taxonomy
to counter my glum thoughts.

Consider the peony, possessed of a hot dry humor
that quelled night visions and melancholia.

Wakeful I pore over the folio pages and
conceive a fondness for kohlrabi –

whose etymology I speculate, comes from the smudged eyes
of Arabic women troweling the desert for roots.

The literal origin – *cavolo rapa*, Italian for kale-turnip, conjures
a marriage of round leaves and bulbous low-down stem.

Then again, *cavolo riscaldato* is a twice-told story,
and *rapa* – a blockhead, the two together – an old tale told by a fool,

surely a history of our times, the willful amnesia,
the dumb acquiescence of fear.

Still I love kohlrabi's form and flavor likened to a
mild sweet turnip savored by peasants and nobility alike.

While other plants were broken to fit the drawing field,
the pungent kohlrabi gives its symmetry whole,

leaves frilled as a noblewoman's ruff (and surely a rascally
green man grins from within the lobed shadows).

The petioles resemble great tree trunks
clasping a vegetal globe.

I could easily hold it in my palm or for that matter,
fling it at night demons binding my thoughts.

The spherical stem bears the deep lumen of a lamp
just snuffed, from brushwork laden with ochre.

The bearded taproot (what foolish Jerome shaken loose
of black earth?) spreads its pale mane towards me

as slowly I nod and for the time being
slump free of both thorn and sorrow.

Bindweed

Days pass like
single-celled organisms.
Once as a child
I measured out drops of
brackish bouquet-
water onto a slide,
lowered the glass slip
and through an eyepiece
witnessed life
inside the smell of death. Now
beneath my bland face a
stagnant heart malingers.

Days pass like dry spores. The
daisies finally crumple.
I may never empty the vase,
like a friend who lost
someone she loved
and kept his flowers
through rot and stench
until the water evaporated and
they shed brown soot on her
table. Years later
the stems still there.
Her belief in the patience
of mourning.
I on the other hand
don't even know who has died.

But one day
I empty the vase just like that.
At least this death's over.
I wander the garden,
observe the persistence of nightshade,
pungent wild mustard and
bindweed that tightens its wiry grip
with the most delicate cord.

Formic Acid

Working late at my desk
I absently lift a hand to my neck,
something crawling there.
Inspect the smeared trail
on my thumb, a red desert ant
reeking of creosote bush.
A huge stench for an insect the
size of a vanishing point which
now approaches,
fills the end of the tunnel
I want to escape.
The light only
a contour of darkness.
The ant bears down
on the soft machinery
of my loneliness.
Freighted with the death
that's not quite done. Mandibles
on the detached head still widen
in threat
toward the tip of my pen.
I finish it off
but the rank odor goes on.
As a child I once walked
on a line of ants
just for something to do.
Then watched them scurry
around their dying.
Horrified at what I had done.
How it could be done
so easily.
Three more ants jitter
across the desk
and fidget with the dead one.
The work is never finished.

Referred Pain

What I don't see
in my aching wrist:
sagebrush, oak, stinking sumac.
October fire-season heat.

    My father before he disappeared.
    The red-tailed hawk
    thirty years ago
    on my gloved right wrist,
    jesses hanging like details
    I could hold onto.
    The first man
    who tamed the raptor
    trained it to kill for him.
    Escaped, the hawk perched
    on our eucalyptus,
    allowed us to come close
    and touch the feathers
    that swiveled around its neck.
    Permitted our stare
    into its keen eye.
    After a few weeks
    of feeding the hawk
    fresh ground chuck
    we drove out into
    the dry scrub hills.
    My father sliced
    through the jesses
    with a dull Exacto blade.
    Just like that.
    The bird flapped awkwardly
    fumbled its perch
    in a nearby black oak.

A few years later
the same disappointment.
My father made

a clumsy escape
that mocked release.
For years I couldn't believe it.
He brought me close to
the hawk
then gave me nothing to
tug us together
but this.

The Bombardier
                – for my stepmother

You write to say that my father can't recall what a
fork means, what a STOP sign signifies. I've met
you only twice,
once in your dark walnut kitchen
before you and my father skipped town
and left no forwarding address.
Then after a thirteen-year silence.

You and my father returned
to clean out his dying mother's apartment
and offered me hard pink candy
from my grandmother's cut-glass dish.
My father rambled on about elves,
raccoons and the long Ontario winter.
He hoped that I was happy to see him.

I said nothing about the years I thought he
might be dead, crazy or maybe
holed up in a convalescent hospital,
bleached green paint blistering the walls. I
didn't ask how you failed
to question the way
my father abandoned his daughters.

You are also a daughter.
Perhaps you urged him to do this.
Recognized the scarcity of his love.
Now you must dress my father. Remind him
where the bathroom is, while he burbles on
about WW II in the South Pacific,
his buddy the bombardier and the lousy food.

You write, *I have to do everything.*
I don't know how to answer. Cannot offer my help.
I consider the horrors of being alone
with a man, companion of twenty-five years

who doesn't even know who you are.
In this way we are alike,
absence our constant companion.

Black Helicopters
                    — Temecula

Dark-eyed juncos chirr
like dislodged bicycle-chains
in the brittlebush.
Wind lifts and drops
ragged curtains of breath.
The metal onion
of the ventilator spins.
The old cabin condemned.
My father never lived here
but still inhabits
the thick blocks of light
that dissolve like lard
in the iron skillet of shadows.
We shared a leaning
toward things emptied of themselves,
the desert, abandoned houses.
I pick my way
across broken windows
collapsed on the pine-plank floor
flannelled with dust.
The swayback roof will finally snap,
the rotten floorboards crumble.
A snake will mimic a braided loaf in
the rusted breadbox.
I look out the window frame,
the exact shape of emptiness. Three
black helicopters approach. My
father has been gone so long and
not even dead.

Off the Richter Scale

This morning the plate jerks north,
finally pitches the tilted cliff into sea.

Mudstone slides from its basalt shelf,
stains the tides ochre.

Dissolves all the history laid down in layers
which now silt the cove with fresh sediment.

For years I drove by and
marked the notched point of land,

sagebrush, buckwheat, Aleppo pine
as ocean fingered the gap from below.

My father, the surrounding space.
How he led me to the natural world

first by attention, then by absence. A
dry pressure beyond measure.

Certain fault lines cannot be predicted. I
never knew what I had done.

Fractures turn molten or slip-strike blindly.
Now at the surface I'm strangely relieved.

The pine at the end of the unnotched cliff
faces the land that is no longer there.

My Father's Birthday

Sometimes he's all around me.
House finches, sparrows.
Broken binoculars,
lens caps lost.
A chipped shovel thrust into
sand near a freeway overpass.

I plant a pine with a friend
for her son who leapt
from the bridge.
Something my father
wouldn't do. Leap
or plant to mark the leap.

My friend, bereft
points and says, he died there
on the freeway.
While I stand dry-eyed in terror.
This is the worst thing
I've ever heard.

Later I watch for the slightest
flick of wings in maples outside
my window.
My father, a birder,
sleeps in a Mennonite
nursing home in Canada.

Sometimes he bawls
over his crow Jack
dead some sixty years ago,
on the phone to my sister
who hasn't seen him
for over thirty years.
Has no idea who we are.

And still I note, today is
his seventy-second birthday.

The Last Thing You See

We pick our way
through burnt gorse
and heather
on animal paths,
follow the black creek
through granite moorland
where Devon shepherds
lit fires to force the green.

The sheared flock
grazes above us.
Bleats back and forth in
hard air.
Wild unseen ponies
nicker and keen beyond
the rise.

Then we separate
each to our quiet.
My daughter mid-stream.
I choose a wind-stunted tree.
On the walk back, she asks,
what were you thinking?

> About my father
> before he left.
> Our journey through England
> when I was sixteen
> a little older than she is,
> and almost happy.

I ask my daughter
the same question.
She answers,

> I watched the water,
> thought maybe you become

      the last thing you see
      before you die.

We consider
what we might want
to witness.
A snowy egret, a cat.
I open the wicket
and close it behind us.

I wish my father's
last glimpse
of the world
would fall on an oak
or yew, any tree
that gathers memory
a long time in one place.

Middle Age and the Rings of Uranus

Astronomers have discovered
that the rings of Uranus
revolving in odd trajectories
swing together with tidal rhythm,
wowing back and forth
in concentric pulses.

Pieces of ice and frozen ammonia
could go on like this
for a million years.

Gradually bits that don't dance
to gravity's synchrony/syncopation
slingshot out into space,
the span of a ring resolved
by elliptical coincidence.

The lifespan of a woman
my age, is also shaped
by pulsations of matter wobbling
around a large planet I've only
begun to view.

Certain events tighten their orbits
or glance off repulsed.
The way I sometimes lurch and falter
around the ones I love,
or dream of constellations
descending within range of my fingers,

the way I encounter my father,
blank gravitational field
that tugs at me
from beneath methane clouds,

or the way I track my mother as
she breaks up, spins out,

and vanishes in the solar wind.
Astronomers liken the universe
to a loaf of bread
that still rises with the energetic
yeast of the Big Bang
and say we're all accelerating at
varying wavelengths
away from each other,
raisins in the loaf.

I also see my life
in terms of the rings
around the green planet,
the improbable ways
we hold together.

Cherimoya

There will be no death-
watch for my father.
No holding his mottled
tobacco-stained hand
no stroking his liver-
spotted skull.
No bedside words.

No comfort gained
from the soluble tone
of my voice that might slip a
thin stream
of water into the thick flower
of his ear.
His wife has withheld
his death from me
until months after the fact.

My father has not appeared in
my dreams as a
Sitka spruce from the far north
where he died or
a paintbrush beside his easel or
a small wise man the size of a
Santa Claus ornament.

For me mourning is a spiny
fruit like the cherimoya
cultivated in my part
of the world at great cost. No
birds or insects
have beaks or proboscises
long enough to pollinate
the monstrous flowers.
The farmer must
painstakingly wheedle
a long-handled brush
into each one.

A Good Compost Needs Water and Air

Standing in the cold garden, my
brown nappy hat
pulled around my ears,
I turn the compost,
survey the winter
sleep of my plants,
mint scruff, spindly thyme,
sightless bulbs, seeds clasped in
damp clay hands,
those spirits
who live underground.
I hear a thin scratching
or guttural crunch
like women chewing on soil
their spittle awakening
minerals and worms.
My blood retreats from
chill fingers like sap.
My head wags a little
between the bushes.
Then shock of air
close by my right ear
as a hawk banks his wings
through the brush,
lands on the chain-link fence.
Yesterday I opened a note from
my stepmother.
He died two months ago.
My father is buried in some
cold Ottawa loam.
The years of his absence
a series of unmarked graves. He
taught me how to live
underground.
Taught me
the slow blind seasons.
The almost bearable

density of silence.
How to steady my arm
beneath hawk talons.
To peel away bark,
pluck violet beetles
from spongy wood
and other odd talents.
Now the hawk's
eyes scrutinize me,
as I kneel to finger
the black grains of dirt
that sifts from the pitched
heart of rot.

Stars Burned in the Sky above Him, Ready to Fall at Any Moment

At the end Galileo turned
away from the *occhiale*
to the *occhialino*, from
telescope to microscope,
and pondered the woody flesh of
the vine, the corpuscular light
taken into the grape.
He said, *The must holds
secret converse with the sun.*

Last night in the dream a man
sat in a closed shrine.
Outside I felt along every wall
for the firm jamb of a door.
I don't know the man
my father, who exiled himself
from his daughters.

Though I heard word of him
from the frozen woods
of Canada. Don't know
if he sent away for spirits.
Apparently he studied
a meager garden, tended certain
plain vegetables.

Galileo also kept a garden
and pruned his vines *beyond
natural diligence*, notes
his friend Bocchardini.
Galileo refined the art
of eel ponds.

When my father died
after losing all knowledge
of pruning shears, wine glasses,

buttons and spoons,
I became like the eels who,
released to the river
couldn't return
to the first ponds.

At the end Galileo spent time
devising a most ingenious
method for measuring

water drops falling
on any given surface.

The father I don't know
sits in a dry lightless place,
ponders my movements
through the walls.
At last I set fire to the rafters.
No other entrance but this,
no other escape.

II. Flung into Silence

November

This is the season
the dead return.
I close the windows,
light a fire
against dread,
but the cranky drafts
of air that finger
the weather-stripping
refuse to speak.

This is the season
the sad astronomer
who trained a shotgun
to the firmament
of his palate
in the Arizona desert,
knocks on the door
that I do not open.

This is the season
of leaky reservoirs,
upended rusted Chevys
and bullet casings.
The season
I turn away from
the leeching cups
and divination knives
of my mother.

This is the season
I finally open the door.
Come in, I say to
all the dead
who have traveled
from as far away
as Australia.

You may as well sit
by the fire and tell me a story.

How to Dress for Death

–for Wolf

He says, *you really must wear the crimson dress,*
fitted bodice, full circle skirt, calf-length, my dear.
An ankle bracelet would be cunning.
For instance, the silver one you found
in a Bangalore bazaar twenty years ago.
I'd skip all the underthings
unless you covet black Venetian lace.
I won't interfere.
The shoes are paramount, though. Red pumps
with heels high enough to tightrope-flex your calves
(ah the muscles on those ponies).
Now my crimson woman, attend to the make-up.
Hibiscus-red lips, kohl-deepened eyes,
but stay clear of the blush.
Tease your hair out to the holy conflagration
it's always craved to be.
Give it all away. And I mean all.
Death will strip you down to the svelte bone anyway.

A Good Death
           – Yellowstone

Years ago
my friend and I agreed
we wanted death
by lightning.
He grew up
with thunderstorms,
St. Elmo's fire,
bolts out of the blue.
Instead I'd only witnessed
sheet lightning
over the desert,
and several strikes
glimpsed from Rome's
Capitoline Hill
where ancient *fulminatores*
divined lightning
for kings.

Now my friend and I live
in different cities.
He has just turned fifty, is
slowly dying
from a virus
that gnaws his brain.
In the summer I visit the
lightning-
charred mountains
whose sky splits open
every day.
I walk and walk.

Clouds heave
like mounds of smoke
pitched over the ridge.
I scuttle away
under thunderclaps

and instantly think
of my friend,
our foolish pact.
Just off the trail
a buffalo is struck, lifted
and dropped by
a crackling bolt.

My friend lies asleep
three states away
and dreams of thunder.
I see him standing
one of many
in the fire-fields
a tall scorched snag
who finally lets go
of the earth,
lies down
in the ashen duff
close to her
when no one is around.

Water on the Moon

> – after the announcement that developers are considering the utilization of ice on the dark side of the moon

A woman swathed
in black cirrus
draws her pocked white
hands to her face,
disclosing the chalk
of her bones
as she keens
in a thin airless voice,
a small dark mirror
flashing from
the back of her skull.

Only the unseen
completes you
only the untouched

she says, this woman who multiplies in
the wells here on earth
we have poisoned.

You know what happens
                      when you break a mirror.

Not Even Angels

flung into silence,

        can tug the suicides back from starvations,
        dances with unfleshed lovers, cathedrals of despair

        back from the cliff's edge at two A.M. off the trail succulent
        with spring
        I walked eight hours ago

        back from the thrill and final fuck-you of the ledge where
        they lined up cigarettes to arrow their death

        back from the salve of nothing, no white tunnel, no
        ascending choirs attendant on final splendor

        back from the place where the cords joining them to life
        snapped like severed ligaments

broken benedictions as they fell into concussions of stone

A String Tied to Each Wrist

Here where I live on a jut of land, the gothic girls
lunge from orange cliffs into blind blue sea.

Alicia, Amber, set off an alphabet of numb birds
who beat the air of my stringent sleep with clipped wings.

Ravens click in the cruel afternoons, so many stopwatches
sniggering dryly behind our backs. Still we do not see it coming.

Streets fray at the edge of land. This is the end of the city
where they finally bolt the loud yap nation

that clamps their heels, muffles their throats with cement.
The earthquake-stricken White Point, fist of land.

They turn their backs and run toward null holding
hands, their wrists joined with a string –

sign of friendship – friend – from the same
Sanskrit root as free, unenslaved.

They bind each other, then loose themselves from the world.
Later gulls, ravens guileless with purpose, descend.

I make a list of all the young dead by suicide in
the past year just a few miles from my home,

children yanked to the vertigo cliffs by
a brief promise of weightlessness.

I scratch a circumference upon the ground
each point on the circle, sorrow. Here is the compass

of what we refuse and what we don't know, how
we're all drawn by loss, cruel borders in air where

Alicia and Amber tether their long
invisible string to our wrists, and pull.

Lunch Tray

She drove her car
straight through the bend
and the road opened,
an old hairpin
that couldn't hold her in place.

I know this road.
The switchbacks
that overlook the channel
between disheveled city and
thin blue island.

A pungent road
tangled with mustard,
artemisia, sage, fennel.
Twice a fox swept across
the road before me like brushfire.

I don't know her name.
The eighteen-year-old
who punched the gas last December.
Drove the blunt shovel
of her car into the gorge.

Could not be found for a month.
Was a perfect student,
they say. A good runner.
Affluent family. Though stick-thin
and always hungry.

Friends left red geraniums there.
Later a lunch tray appeared
a tilted gravestone
in the chalky earth,
brim with letters to the dead girl.

To the Prevailing Wind

At first there was no sign of you unless you were skulking
in night subways or pooled curbside in rectangular canyons
of morning along the streets, until light gust, you teased
a woman's indigo skirt or a man's black pant leg, flipped
a newspaper page in the hands of Stavros who sold bags of oranges
on Eighth Avenue. Idly you mussed the hair of hundreds
walking lower Manhattan or plucked leaves from balcony gardens where
tomatoes hung swollen with one last drop of summer.
You eddied around the flashing heels of children on playgrounds and
swooped back down into subterranean pistons of air.

From where I stood on another coast there was no sign of you
when it happened, happens, (present tense perpetual
of the looped event) no sign of you when the sky drops, you
don't rouse or speak out of the rubble, nothing.
As is often your way. A man on the eighty-seventh floor sees
pieces of paper flutter by *gently on a breeze*.
Now you show up and lift all the used and unused days from
thousands of calendars, profit plans, losses.

A stark-eyed reporter snatches up papers, reels off letterheads
and looks for a distracted moment as if she wants to
collate the flurry of papers, some of which you carry
north toward my friend Maggie who lives in a loft
on Thirty-Sixth street, floor 12B, once an old button factory
where she finds and collects random vellum sheets on her balcony.
Though this is not, she tells me, as grim
as the acid stench you carry in your shocked breath.

The Disappearance of Vanilla

I walk a desolate plain
turn east near a bridge
twisted and melted
by unspeakable wind
and enter an empty city
where I hear a voice,
Sometimes we die of silence.
I encounter no one
in the streets
nor in my office.
Inhabitants
are assigned spaces
of equidistant isolation.
In the hallway
I'm startled by
a young Japanese woman
with green skin
and a fragrance of vanilla.
I put my arm around
her shoulders. Other
women, men and children
huddle close to me.
I say *I will protect you*
but their limbs flicker
around me.
*After Hiroshima, all
vanilla orchids in Pacific islands
disappeared.*

Ossa, Woman's Bones

> – an abandoned village in Umbria

I enter the village
of moss-stubbled
paving stones,
grassy walls
cropped by goats,
the prickly fingers
of blackberry cane
poking through
barred cellar windows,
casements and eaves.

Vines pry shutters
from loose stucco
and trail new shoots
into luminous rooms
paved with cracked
citrine tiles.
Curtains are shredded
by mildew,
nails bleed rust.

The old office of records
unlit by a single
corroded light-bulb,
vomits papers
like folds of tripe,
pages of elegant
signatures that mean
nothing to me
though they might signify a
village of kin.

Here even silence falls
into slow decay.
In another room

a wooden brush
on a chipped marble sill
offers alphabets etched
by tiny black beetles
and in the pigs' bristles
a cursive of dry red curls. I
don't recognize
the woman by her hair
though she's almost familiar.
Connected to
the stones and burials,
the single femur, ribs
and vertebral couplings
a farmer unearthed
while enlarging a cave below
the village
to store his oak vats of wine.
The feminine long bone
carved with Etruscan letters.

He also dug up a bowl,
a mirror, a bronze comb. I
can't find the rocks
set on her bones
to keep them
from wandering.
Even after I leave
the village the light harp of
her skeleton
rings in my ears.
Her white minerals
green my words.

Caps of Pure Silk

My great-grandmother Annunziata
loved the slant of perfumed mirrors in
half-lit hotel corridors, stockinged with
dust, her paste gems heaving upon the
acquired breath of linen.

Her ancestors locked the true gems
in a dark vault licked by saltwater. Topaz,
jasper, sapphire, ruby, diamonds lit from
within. Uncut opals burning. And all the
furtive gold chains, unclasped.

(The courtesans in this city
are not allowed to wear gold,
silver, or silk as part of their dress. . .
except for caps of pure silk.
– Sumptuary Laws, Venezia 1562)

Indolence runs in the family. Even my
grandfather frittered his fortune, languidly
counting his last coins
while others slept in ochre rooms
or twined in the hissing wheat of midday.

My mother says, the blood of the Prince
of Torlonia runs in our veins! Or falters
there like paint seeping into wet plaster,
our frescoed past a ceiling that flakes
mildewed graces, winds, angels upon us.

Dark grit of grandeur, pursed lips of
pleasure, royalty, royalty, *remolata*.
My fine inheritance comes to nil.
And the old villa closed now, staggers
beneath caustic rains, raw sun, stink

of the dead deprived even of final rites,
the coins snatched from beneath their tongues
by kin in *flagrante delicto*, the hundred- year-old
wisteria razed to make way
for a dance-floor that never was built.

Only the caps of silk are left in a tattered
trunk in the old seamstress' attic.
Only the unnetted pearls that scurried
beneath the bed. The silver chains stolen
by crows in the sumptuary hours.

The Bright New Dress and the Book About Jungles

A fat moon glared through blue eucalyptus,
sent spiky shadows across our faces.
My mother moaned singsong *non posso scendere,*
I can't come down, la bella luna,
the beautiful moon, she is calling me.

That winter night my mother climbed into
the tree house, my secret hideout stashed
with dolls, dead beetles and Oreos.
Rocked herself in the same raft of branches
that bore me down the Amazon River.

My father carried me into the house
where I crept into my mother's studio steeped
in the odor of turpentine rags.
On the easel her unfinished painting –
a stone Madonna breaking down into flesh.

From the unlit window I watched
two men in white, strap my mother
into a shirt with sleeves too long for her.
Then she was taken into a van.
I'll get you for this, she snarled at

no one in particular and everyone present.
I'd just celebrated my birthday
when I was happy to be a number divisible
by both odd and even.
Whole systems were based on ten.

My mother gave me a bright new dress
she'd sewn herself and my father
gave me a book all about jungles.

Cara Mamina

For years I wrote letters sank
my words like nets weighted
with small lead fish
around your iron bathysphere
embedded in the ashen
Tyrrhenian sea floor.
As if I could haul you up with
something so tenuous,
my purse seine of love
around your expulsion of me.

Sinking, I peered through
the round clamped window
to see you within:
your easel, the oil paintings
of garish Madonnas,
the noxious sting of turpentine
which leaked from the
riveted seams of your madness.

I lived there with you
for a long time, listened
to stories of catacombed grief
your father's cruel scowl
your mother's calm suffocations
your botched suicides.
Though you didn't want death.
Instead you meant to
sever your hands.

You wanted to suture mine
to your empty wrists
but my hands refused
to take up brushes and paint,
refused to make fists against
the thick submersible walls.
You wrenched out black

livid-rooted   hair,
curled   into   a   ball
tighter than the lead shot
that secured my weight belt.
You cursed me because
I finally chose to surface.

Sometimes when I visit
I lay my hand against your sphere
as if I were stroking
your bald head,
or a steel plate in the skull,
a metal so unforgiving
I know you will never feel me.

Swarms

The first swarm hung
like iron shavings
from my horseshoe magnet
when I was ten.
Moiled on the branch
of an ancient oak
in the Cuyamaca mountains.
My father beside me, pointed
with his burled walking stick,
and compared the buzz to WW
II bombers.

Twenty years later
a swarm agitated
the eaves of my mother's
Umbrian house
while she slept off anger
in the hot afternoon.
My sister and I also groggy
with spent rage, slumped in the red
metal garden chairs.
In our mother's studio, painted bees
dried on her recent self-portrait.

Three more years
before the next swarm
in a friend's summer garden,
congealed fist of sex
on the lemon tree,
queen at the center
encrusted with drones
workers attendant to hiving lust as
we consider what lies couched in
the long afternoons
of our marriages.

Now nine years later
the bees' condensed flight
mimics sub-atomics,
cloud chamber scribbles
that mark the fields
of the invisible.
My husband and I gather up
our picnic and watch
the bees clump,
understanding that
the world as we know it has
ended again.

III. A Lantern of Air

A Night Where Sounds Ranged Far Beyond Hearing

– for Ursa

When the howl
went out of the house
the walls lost their fur
and the windows
no longer twitched
with the branches
of dark impenetrable woods,
yellow eyes and moon
a coin under night's dense tongue.
We bared our teeth
bristled nape of memory,
footfalls clattered
claws tapping a field of ice while
a hundred small stones slid all at
once from my lap, clinked
against the small teeth
of the hours and my hands became
tuning forks of loss.
The wolf was gone,
the house a bone pith sucked dry.
She taught me what it meant
to be ravened by teeth
to grunt seasons,
to lick the rump of love.
I knew that the smell
of joy was more
than a transfusion of days,
knew that the catheter of routine
thinned her blood,
the wolf I buried
my face in.
The red bandages
always unwound,
her cracked footpads
would not touch earth
but her eyes at the last were open.

Dog

Yesterday I planted a tree on my old dog's grave.
The place she often slept, trembling with dreams of tundra.

Wolves scratch at the back door of my sleep.
I don't let them in though my heart slips its catch.

A woman brought me a knobby pomegranate,
dwarf fruit that cracked like a small casket open.

I've never liked rubies or drops of blood.
When my daughter cut her arm, I had to look away.

The world frays, a bandage of stained white gauze.
Still I know how to dress a wound.

Please Fined him soon

says the round note I find in
my mailbox today –
                Lost Dog
                      mail Dog golded lab
                    dog Skinny full
                lankth tail named Benjy

In my room the computer says
unimplemented trap

and *forgotten your password?*
press here if you wish to receive a hint.

When I click the button
two dead dogs comes up.

Ah – the wolf and the mutt, my beloved ghosts
who gain me entry to nets of words.

Ursa, Cosmo and now I think, Benjy
where have you wandered?

Some little child is devoted to you.
My daughter calls up from downstairs.

I'm working, I answer, mildly annoyed at
our living dogs who at this moment

rankle the door to the garage
and yelp uncontrollably.

Mom! A dog followed me home.
Some big sloppy lunk named Mack

friendly as a cartoon dog
is galumphing through our garage.

His big mottled head bangs like an anvil
against the washing machine.

I'm downstairs now.
What is that? my daughter asks, *a pit bull?*

I don't know, smelling the great
happy smell of dog urine.

I find the address on his tag,
take him home and later back in my room,

close my eyes, as the computer hums
and I smell the damp fur of Ursa.

I would follow her anywhere now.
Dogs have that gift – to track

the scent of something
they cannot see.

Milk Then Bone
                 – a lullaby

green then black
cord then cut
fire, ash

moist then dry
light then muck
moon, moon

taste then bland
fontanelle, skull
sea, sea

spoon then needle
suck then clutch
open, close

blood then brine
fill then empty
ma, maw

clear then blank
many then one
one, one

Grazia's Teeth

In this country
lost teeth tucked under the pillow
emerge silver coins in
the morning.
The tooth-fairy stages this magic.
My young daughter
calls her a cat-tooth-fairy
and informs me
that I'm not her real mother.
Cats are her kin.
I've always admired
the wild in my daughter,
an agile beauty like that
of felines that saunter or stalk.

In another country
my daughter befriends a girl who
loses her tooth in the pizza.
*Will you put it under
your pillow? and do
the fairies leave
coins?*
The child answers,
*Nonna hammers my teeth
in the door for a blessing,
want to see?*
We walk to her grandmother's
small stone house.

Grazia's teeth shine
in the grooves and knotholes
of pine like tiny shells,
pearl mushrooms in gray wood,
or half-moons that rise
in the fingernails of a princess
embedded within the tree.

As we enter the house
I think of my own baby teeth
gone long ago, replaced
by more sensible ones.
My daughter still has teeth to
lose and lives by magic.

Brussels Sprouts in Limbo

After we die, my daughter's friend says, *if*
we're not too good or too bad
we go to limbo where we must eat
Brussels sprouts for seven years
if that is what we refused on earth.

Then we ascend to heaven
(where hopefully there are no vegetables). I
consider what I've refused:
white bread, sugar, milk, meat
and picture myself as a plump carnivore

eating my way toward god.
Beatitude means chewing death,
savoring the taste of one's enemy, Lima
beans, or the messy beast of sex.
I polish the spoons but do not sit at the table.

Fear is a stern butler.
I still worry which fork goes on the outside,
which way the knife should be turned.
For every pleasure
there is an etiquette of terror.

But today I will turn to my love
over raspberry pots-de-crème
and yank the tablecloth onto the floor,
dishes, silverware settings flung wide
in the bright percussion of desire.

The Origins of Language

Pressing my ear to the earth
I hear groundwater creep one-tenth
of a mile per year,
hear quakes before they convulse
and jump the slim beak
on the paper cylinder
to jagged black arcs
of astonishment.
Hear the noise of the city
my lover inhabits,
pressing my ear to his body,
my ear to his ear,
aural mirror to mirror,
seismicity a measure
of subterranean words
mouthed by a populace
whose tongues lie under
injunctions of shale and basalt.
Instruments on Mount Wilson detect
every twitch and suspiration.
Pressing my ear to his throat
the larynx where utterance
subducts just short
of the magmic tongue.
My ear to his chest,
clenched heart unclenched.
To his pulse marked by
black ink scrawls
on the white seismographic wrist. To
the mute flesh pen
as it speaks its first
halting letters, then
proudly stutters slippage,
hums and howls and lifts
into ancient stone song.

The Best Time to Plant

When the first monarch flashes
across my yard this September,
advertises singular orange
and black inedibility
conferred by milkweed,
my appetite for the invisible leaps
like a compass needle or tiny magnet
within the butterfly's brain,
awakens the old urge south
where it's never been before,
this journey that takes
generations of monarchs to complete. I
change course and no one knows. Gray
whales will soon descend
from the Bering Sea, hugely pregnant.
White-crowned sparrows already dapple
the thicket of red honeysuckle. Then
rain. The ants move in,
nest in the Garland stove's back-burner.
This is the best time to plant
in my part of the country.
Leaves may not multiply with
the blatant redundance of summer
but all winter long the white roots will
spread and finger the way.

Buzz Saw and Mockingbird

Italo Calvino once resolved to write down
every moment in a single day.

The mind like a buzz saw spins in its groove
and builds a house at the same time.

If you're marking
each moment how do you live?

These plain days become an almanac
of signs I may open to any forecast.

My daughter's copper hair folds to her neck like
wind-combed grass that shows us the land.

Once a man saw the name of Allah
written by bees in a honeycomb.

A mockingbird predicts insects in clipped rye
and flashes her semaphore wings.

A Shaker woman invented the circular saw.
I marvel at how she did it, and then I understand.

The sun cuts deeply into the sea, throws a tooth
of light, and halts a thin second for nightfall.

La Gruta

Today I wade through a stone tunnel in central Mexico,
waist-deep in hot mineral springs,

half-blind in the thin light until it widens within
limestone walls, a domed cave weeping sulfur.

A tamarind woman of many folds lounges in water
the blue of my first milk

upon the lips of my infant daughter who, grown now,
will soon leave home.

Sometimes I'm sorry to grow old. A friend says
once you reach forty your voice will signify more than

your looks, while another friend says, women soften with age,
we are settling, my dear, like sediment.

We splash and sputter in the dim grotto. A
lank old man floats on his back,

drifts and slowly revolves north toward
the uninhabited mountains of silence.

Funnel Spider

She works
her spinnerets
in the coiled earth,
knits a mesh
that draws me down
through a lightless
tunnel of waiting.
A gauze, mute womb.
Limitless as the body's
red speech hushed,
as the children
I will no longer bear.

She asks me
to slough
little vanities,
errors gone dry.
In certain parts
of the world
a woman past child-bearing
strikes fields fallow,
unmans a lover,
turns wine to vinegar.
Better not cross
or ignore her.

The spider knows
where to set the lines.
Where to bend
the weave,
work the heft
of hunger.
In summer
the sage hills flicker
with her dusty
shirred silk,

the pale
webbed mouths
of her prose.

This new
codex hums
in my body.
Words for tissues
of recollection,
lunar fluency,
small secretions of
faith.
The way pulse is weft
to death's still warp,
and her deepest gift –
where to place
the invisible center,
how to hold absolutely
nothing.

The Finishing Stitches

Today while I sew
my daughter's pointe shoes I
misplace the scissors. When
I was a girl
my mother's teeth
were keen enough to snap
the taut thread.
How did she do that
with all those pins
between her lips
pricking the air?

I grind my teeth
on the doubled pink thread
without success.
My bite is not as sharp
as my mother's, nor as final
as thirteen years
of estrangement.
My mother,
accomplished seamstress,
couldn't forgive me
the stitches that ran
against the bias.

I'm left to do
the finishing, tack
the edges down,
tie off with three knots along
the raw slant of Freed
ribbons
that fasten the pointe shoes.
Tonight my daughter will
dance the Snow Queen,
deftly stitch her own
steps to the darkness beyond
the spotlight
that holds her in its beam.

The Quinceañera
– Los Angeles

All night cumbia, gallons of goat stew,
mole, tortillas, wine and beer in honor of
lovely Yadira, whose crisp black ringlets shimmer
like sateen ribbons curled by scissors.

Yadira, fifteen-year-old-
white-satin-lace-beaded-bride, presides
over the party, ripens among the cowboy hats
like a spray of Annunciation lilies under the full moon,

dances with brother Jaime in smart
Marine dress-uniform and spit-perfect black
patent-leather shoes that snap to
the Honduran conjunto rhythm.

Later eight children dance a Strauss waltz and
even the long lost brother Enrique calls from
God knows where,
while her mother Blanca shimmies

as only she can, her newest baby Lourdes
asleep in the house, her mouth round
as a wedding ring, tiny fists primed for nightmares
that won't get away with esa's joy.

The older sister who picked a purple VW
instead of a quinceañera gawks at the three-tier rosette
piped cake with miniature ballroom staircases
arcing down from each side

while at the pinnacle a tiny Yadira oversees
her sugar kingdom that we will consume tonight.
My pale teenage daughter and I
sit wide-eyed the only Anglos
out on the sweat-spicy crowded patio

while guys in the corner quip *here comes
the virgin march* as young girls perform
their manless dance.

The loopy awnings overhead and
light bulbs strung in tropic constellations
billow and jangle a memory of
Dzilam de Bravo two decades ago.

Bacardi and coke, dirty-jokes-among-women-nights,
the first time I danced the cumbia easy-hips-small-
stepping-frying-fish- in-fifty-gallon-drums-of-oil-
nights.

When Yadira asks my daughter, will you
have a quinceañera? she shakes her head
and we exchange a glance from our city
where pageant rarely breaks out.

Then I hear it hum under my daughter's voice, like
a distant carnival or saint's parade
with vivid Madonna rocking on monkish shoulders,
her bright still undisplayed revelries

about to stride from side streets into the
center of her independence dance, just
under her breath this revel-church- rich-
feast-of-ripening-night.

Three Breaths

The sea crackles
around me with unseen
brine shrimp

like a staticky old
radio picking up
China's tomorrow.

Sound travels farther
underwater. Memory
glides amphibious.

My husband calls out
turtle, sea turtle!
and when I swim toward him

the beast surfaces close by
one left eye watchful of my two.
I float among algae boas

while the turtle
draws breath and descends
with the same elegance

expressed by an equation,
curving between grace
and the beauty of necessity.

The flippers that are wings.
The carapace that sinks
like a dark hunchback moon.

My husband and
my daughter
plunge slowly down

behind the turtle
into the teeming water
of their lives.

    A weaker
swimmer, I stay at
  the surface and
  admire all three

dive through deepening
blue thermocline like
bodies slowly immersed in dye.

The turtle swivels, coasts
beneath
a coral lip of darkness.

In our blood we hold
the same share of salt
to water.

Not a day passes
without fear I will lose
them or myself.

When they rise on
the last breath
they return to me

from the ultramarine
sleep of all that is lost.
My husband exhales, says,

Did you notice?
the turtles take . . .
then my daughter

holds up three fingers,
breaths. And they laugh

because they are one
thought together.
I who did not count
think, one breath to clear

one breath to take
the measure of things
and one breath to carry
down into the yielding
lungs of the sea – a bell
of breath, a lantern of air.

The View from Tahquitz Peak

> *I want my ashes*
> *scattered here on this ridge*
> *between worlds.*

My daughter and I
walk the familiar
South Ridge trail,

peer through cloud-break at
the end
of each switchback.

We swing back and forth
up the mountain
a mother-daughter pendulum,

decide to go further than
ever before.
No one else on the path

this New Year's Day. We
ride out the breath of
incoming storm:

inhale west —
cedar, fir and pine
forest lifts and thrashes,

exhale east —
high desert troughs
blur with sand.

We know the way
between these two
up to icy granite

then across to the sheltering
hollow my daughter calls
a place of small spirits.

She is sixteen and I'm
middle-aged.
We don't know

the way that
now ascends
a wild flank before us.

This is the kind of grandmother
mountain who chips at us
as if we were chert

and sharpens us to arrows.
My daughter quickens
then waits but I say

go on without me.
I can't keep up,
am always decades

behind.
Two switchbacks
and she's gone.

People have
fallen from
this mountain.

I plod and stare down at
precise gravel,
beetles edified by cold,

cleat marks of others
on the path.
A sudden lightness arrives.

Twisted limber pine
stands firm in its crevice.
Old old tree flings

rain on my face.
I belong right here. Crusted
snow underfoot.

At last I see my daughter
at the cloud-wrapped summit
cradled among boulders

like a damp seed
about to split its husk.
I climb up to meet her.

Lookout tower behind us,
arms around each other
we can't see a thing.

www.ingramcontent.com/pod-product-compliance
Lightning Source LLC
Chambersburg PA
CBHW052115070526
44584CB00017B/2489